# AND  ID:
# TH E

*Your innermost questions answered.*

*Published by*
**THE BOSGO PRESS**

# PAUL BURA

*WWW.PAULBURA.CO.UK*

•

ISBN 0 906786 23 1

ISBN 0 906786 23 1

Previous books by Paul Bura:
*Just Another Poet*
*Mustn't Dent The Memory*
*Behind The Joker*
*From Under The Stairs*
*The Coming Of The Giants*
*The Space Between The Syllables*
*In The End Love Is All There Is*
*The Oak On The Plain*
*Joeb – Servant of Gaia*
*Quest For Contact*
*The Drunk On The Train*
*Stepping To The Drummer*

Published by
THE BOSGO PRESS
12, Gongl Rhedyn,
Cemaes Bay,
ANGLESEY LL67 OHY

# INTRODUCTION

Dowsing is the ancient art of divination, either using
the pendulum, L-rods or swivel-stick or whatever
form that suits your psychic make-up. Of course you
need neither of these: one can develop the
'twitching-nose' or the 'clenching and unclenching of
the hand', or that great sense of simply 'knowing'. All
of these methods are simply tapping into the Universal
Overself. A part of the unconscious mind. Whatever
method you use can lead you to the correct quotation
for **you.**
     I have called this book: **AND LOVE SAID...**
**The Oracle (of Love and Change)** because that is
what it is. A **TOOL** to help and guide you.

When I started this book I came at it with the
thought that I would just substitute the word 'LOVE'
for the various philosophical sayings and statements
that the great masters of wisdom said be they
Christian, Buddhist, Muslim. etc. or the great poets
and philosophers.

> **EXAMPLE:** Jesus said, love your enemies.

> I would just substitute the word/name 'Jesus'
> for the word 'LOVE'. Thus...

> **And LOVE said:** love your enemies, etc.

For a while all went well. But I kept thinking of
things that Love would say (or hoped it would say).
And I kept writing more and more. Granted things that
I had heard the great masters say **must** have become
lodged in my subconscious mind but it became more
than that. It started to pour out of me in such a rush.

Then it would stop. And then start again. I had to re-read the material and sometimes I didn't always understand what I had written as it was kind of 'abstract' sounding, material that I hadn't heard before, or, at least, put in that context. But I didn't want to interfere with it, tamper with it, so I left it like it was. Sometimes I would try and lengthen it or shorten it to make more sense of it but I ended up leaving it alone  Somebody out there must **need** it. There are those of you who may think that ego has gotten hold of me. Well, I honestly don't blame you.

I try to live up to the teachings but like everybody else I sometimes fail miserably.

## AND LOVE SAID:  was not written in
the conventional sense and I apologize for the odd mis-quote that may have lodged in my unconscious mind (if mis-quote it was), it is what it is. And I'm sure that if **you** were to settle down with pen and paper and put yourself in love's Pilot Seat you would come up with some original material too. But is it original? I doubt it. But if you settle down with LOVE on your mind. Well, who knows. Sometimes I've found myself responding to an original quote as if to clarify it. I make no apologies for that.

This book is **ideal** for **DOWSERS.** It is finely balanced in multiples of 9 which brings a certain ambience to it. By the simple process of elimination you can find the quote that you can rest your day on, or week, or month, or whatever.

The book is in 5 Sections. One should dowse for the correct Section for **you.** When you have achieved this dowse for your page number: Each Section has 9 pages (nine fives are forty five,

*five plus four equals NINE. Get it?) Section.1. has, of
course, pages 1 to 9. Having dowsed for your
PAGE number, NOW dowse for your quote.*

*EXAMPLE: Page.7. of Section.1. has 8 .quotes
(Quotes can vary from 2 to 9, or even 10 per page).
These 8 quotes number from 50 to 57. Now dowse
for your number. If your quote is 51 then your quote
should read:* "Within silence there is the beauty that
roars." *Or if, for example, the pendulum swings
'yes' for quote 56 then it should read:* "All is as it
should be: just a murmer on the lake," *then you have
found your quote.* It really is as simple as that.

*You may wish to ask the book a specific
question, like: "Why am I so tired?," or "I'm
grieving, please help me." "I am in conflict and I'm
so depressed." The quotes will offer their advise
whatever you ask. Even an obscure answer, left gently
on the mind, will offer help.*

### METHOD (1) FOR THE NON-DOWSER.

*Take a pendulum (if you don't have one a simple
cotton thread through a metal nut or ring will do).
To operate your pendulum: firstly start a gentle swing
to and fro away from you., whilst at the same time
posing the question to yourself, or out loud: "Please
balance me! Please balance me! Please balance me!"
The pendulum will then start to swing in a circle.
Wait for it to stop and start briefly to swing the
other way. The pendulum will either stop or start to
swing gently away from you again. If it stops then
start the swing (oscillation) again. Then ask the
question: "Which way is 'yes' for me?" The
pendulum will then swing either clock-wise or anti
clock-wise for your 'yes'. The reverse swing is of*

*course your 'no'.*

## THE L-ROD METHOD(2)
*Take a wire coat hanger and straighten it out. Then
bend it into an L shape so that it fits your hand. The
wire should be about 15" long, about 38cms. Hold it
loosely but firmly away from you in a straight line.
Then ask your question. Ask the rod which section is
for YOU: 1,2,3,4 or5. The rod will then sway over
(either way) at the appropriate number. When you
get to your number, then ask for your page
number...and so on until you arrive at your quote.*

*In Section.1. you will find the page numbers from
1–9 and the section numbers 1–5. Place your finger
(or use a pointer) on section number.1. and then
2, and so on until you get a responce with either rod
or pendulum. Do the same with the page numbers.*

## THE 'HANDS ON' METHOD(3)
*Open the Oracle at Section.1. Place both hands on
the Oracle and ask your question. Having asked your
question with eyes closed, open book at random with
eyes still closed. When you have selected your page,
no matter what section you open it at, stab your
finger down on a page, this then is your quote,
though not as accurate as if you were to DOWSE for
your answer. It is thought best to read the WHOLE
page if the answer to your question is rather woolly.*

*MY GRATEFUL THANKS TO:*
John Cuninghame. Peter and Diane Castle.
Sylvia Porthouse. David Russell. Hilda Bell.
Hanne Jahr and Steffie Sorrell and many
more.

*FOR THOSE WHO FIND IT DIFFICULT TO VISUALISE*

# SECTION

# ONE

**2.** DOWSE *DOWN* FOR *PAGE* NUMBER:

1

2

3

4

1.*SECTION* NUMBER DOWSE *ACROSS*: 1  2  3  4  5

6

7

8

9

# AND LOVE SAID...

1.  *And Love said:* Wisdom stands or falls by her own actions.

2.  *And Love said:* come to me all you who are weary and burdened, and I will give you rest. Put on my yoke and learn from me. For I am gentle and humble in heart and you will find rest for your souls. For my yoke is easy and my burden is light.

3.  *And Love said:* You must choose between having a good tree with good fruit and a rotten tree with rotten fruit. For you can tell a tree at once by its fruit.

4.  *And Love said:* Do not try to measure me you will only fail.

5.  *And Love said:* I require no door to enter – I live always everywhere.

6.  *And Love said:* Just as the clouds hide the glory of the sun the clouds of doubt and delusion hide my glory from your understanding.

7.  *And Love said:* Cultivate Love first and all things will follow.

8.  *And Love said:* Love never changes, it's only one's conception of it that changes.

9.  *And Love said:* All things flow from me and to me, expanding as they go hither and dither.

10.   *And Love said:* Nurture me in your pain for I will never let go of you.

11.   *And Love said:* Carry me always in your top pocket and let me out occasionally for I will comfort you.

12.   *And Love said:* I dwell in the highest points and also the lowest. It is up to you to search for me. But know that I am always here.

13.   *And Love said:* Remember this, I am eternal and death means nothing to me, only change.

14.   *And Love said:* And remember this also: do not fear change (death) for change happens every day of your life but you survive and grow stronger and wiser and more loving.

15.   *And Love said:* Honour everything that lives, for *everything* surely does, without exception.

16.   *And Love said:* I am all that exists. Nothing is created but an extension of me.

17.   *And Love said:* Time is a tool that is frequently misunderstood. Time is not your master but your servant.

18.   *And Love said:* you may lose sight of me but I *never* lose sight of that which I created, for I am an extension of it.

19. *And Love said:* Your concept of time binds
you. This moment in which you live is the
moment of freedom. Cut the bonds and live it.

20. *And Love said:* Your parents are your parents,
you may love them or not. But *they* brought
you here and one day you will be a parent too.
Is it too much to ask that you love your
children as they, no doubt, loved you? They
will love you no matter what and in the harsh
reality of life, it is *this* that bears you up. You
would have to stray a long way from the path
of Love for them to desert you, wouldn't you
say?

21. *And Love said:* Do not follow where the path
may lead. Go, instead, where there is no path
and leave a trail.

22. *And Love said:* Do not comment when anger
speaks. Let it dispel in its own time and in its
own way. Anger, like a disease, contaminates
and inflames. Be silent.

23. *And Love said:* Tolerate and be silent. Teach
by example.

24. *And Love said:* Follow me throughout all the
great religions. For I am there at their centre.
If not, do *not* follow me!

25. *And Love said:* Let not emotion guide your
intuition. But if it does, do it anyway and learn
from your mistakes.

26.  *And Love said:* I am the balance throughout
     the whole of creation even that that I am yet
     to create. Those that tip the balance slide away
     from me...and into my arms. For I can love
     them all, and loving all brings them back into
     balance.

27.  *And Love said:* Forgiveness is Love. No
     matter how long it takes. People change.
     They do, you know. No matter how long
     it takes. A year. A lifetime. Two lifetimes!

28.  *And Love said:* I can show you wonders
     beyond the stars. But the one great wonder
     is *you!* Or Myself. They are one and the
     same.

29.  *And Love said:* Surrender to me for the war is
     over!

30.  *And Love said:* Cultivate love not sex for we
     all get old. Sex for its own sake, like any
     desire, binds you. Build a balance between the
     two and you will be free.

31.  *And Love said:* To seek freedom(love) is the
     only driving force I know. Freedom to fly off
     into that infinity out there. Freedom to
     dissolve; to lift off; to be like the flame of a
     candle which, in spite of being up against the
     light of a billion stars, remains intact, because
     it never pretended to be more than what it is:
     a mere candle.

(5)

32. *And Love said:* And where does fear come into the equation? They that fear the Infinite instead of loving the Infinite fear's 'fear' itself. You cannot do both. Love and fear do not equate.

33. *And Love said:* A tree that is undernourished. Yet still it puts out it's branches toward the Light. I could not love it more than if it were healthy.

34. *And Love said:* Laughter is the balm of the Gods. If laughter is not present than neither am I.

35. *And Love said:* Ruling by fear is a subjection. Ruling by Love is an obligation.

36. *And Love said:* Love your enemies.

37. *And Love said:* I come to restore the law of Love. In the end it is all that exists. I love you and you love me. It is that simple.

38. *And Love said:* You and I are the true soul-mates. We are scattered throughout the vastness of the universe. Yet we are still One. I am attempting to make simplicity into complexity...or is it the other way round?

39. *And Love said:* The Infinite is incapable of making a mistake. But *you* are.

40. *And Love said:* You are the sum-total of all that has gone before. You have nobody to blame.

41.   *And Love said:* Nothing really matters because nothing really exists. Only I exist!

42.   *And Love said:* The area of space that I take up is small. But *you* are enormous!

43.   *And Love said:* Perfume cannot hide who you are. The body cannot hide who you are. Fine clothes cannot hide who you are. But what you *do* gives you away.

44.   *And Love said:* I am the only thing to cling on to when the wreckage floats by. Hold on to me tightly.

45.   *And Love said:* Give me a try. You have nothing to lose and everything to gain.

46.   *And Love said:* Cultivate simplicity and not complicity. In complicity there is inconsistency. In simplicity there is truth.

47.   *And Love said:* True love is when you can take the rough with the smooth and take each other the way they are, warts and all.

48.   *And Love said:* The trees, animals, plants and insects are all your brothers and sisters. Love and respect them for their different ways. For *all* are aware of *you,* even the rocks!

49.   *And Love said:* I am with you, even unto the end of the world.

50.   *And Love said:* Within every soul there is a pattern, or chord, belonging to no one but you. The pattern only changes when you begin to sing a different song.

51.   *And Love said:* Within silence there is the beauty that roars.

52.   *And Love said:* It is said that I come and I go. I am *always* there only you don't recognize me.

53.   *And Love said:* Father, forgive them for they know not what they do.

54.   *And Love said:* They who know the law and break it, their's is the greater sin. They who are unaware of the law, and break it, who can blame them? But they who refuse to learn the law are out-of-control and therefore need my love.

55.   *And Love said:* You may hide from me but you may as well hide from that which you breathe.

56.   *And Love said:* All is as it should be: just a murmur on the lake.

57.   *And Love said:* You must learn this or you cannot progress: life is eternal. There is no beginning and no end but a continuation. I will not let you down, never desert you, though you may think that I do. Let me in to your heart and I will prove it.

58.   *And Love said:* You have to 'lose face' just once in your life, maybe even many, in your search for me. Admit that you were wrong and it becomes easier until you have no need to 'lose face' any more, because you will have found me. It takes a brave man in the sight of his fellows to admit you were wrong. How bad is that?

59.   *And Love said:* You cannot reach God through the intellect but through me only. Bring your intellect along for the ride though, it might be useful along the way. But don't be surprised if you lose it!

60.   *And Love said:* It does not matter a bit if you have no faith in me or in God. Have faith in yourselves, for who are you really? Each of you is Divinity, whether you know it or not.

61.   *And Love said:* Above all, do every act as an offering to the Infinite, without being elated by success or dejected by defeat; this gives the poise and equanimity for sailing through the waters of the ocean of life.

62.   *And Love said:* Service to man/womankind is a short-cut to the Infinite. But be warned: service to one's ego via the same route will be found out! Unless you do it with love it doesn't count!

63.   *And Love said:* Remember, with each act of love and service you are nearing the divine; with each act of hate and grab you're moving farther and farther away.

64.  *And Love said:* For the clinically depressed I
     say: I LOVE YOU. I LOVE YOU. I LOVE YOU.
     For the maniacally depressed I say:
     I LOVE YOU. I LOVE YOU. I LOVE YOU.

65.  *And Love said:* For those that grieve I say:
     *nothing* is ever lost. Life is eternal. Take comfort
     in this knowledge. Yet comfort you do *not* take.
     What then do you want? To banish death? Or the
     process of dying. Each of you must part at one
     time or another. "But why now?" you ask. Oh
     why indeed.

66.  *And Love said:* For those that fear death because
     it might bring those that they fear. Take heart,
     for no-one is seen unless they wish it. Even then,
     I will surround them like a shield!

67.  *And Love said:* You must 'lose face' in order to
     'gain face'.

68.  *And Love said:* You cannot hide from that that
     witnessed it.

69.  *And Love said:* If you do not keep pace with your
     companions perhaps it's because you are hearing a
     different drummer. Step to the music that *you*
     hear no matter how measured or far away.

70.  *And Love said:* Step for six months in my shoes
     and experience the way I see and feel.

71.  *And Love said:* And what one amongst you will
     cast the first stone?

# SECTION TWO

———

72.  *And Love said:* Give Love a chance, give me an
     even break. What do you say?

73.  *And love said:* When you realise the truth that I
     *am* the Truth then and only then can we
     celebrate your coming home.

74.  *And Love said:* Don't you see: Love has no
     labels. None.

75.  *And Love said:* Forgive us our trespasses as we
     forgive them *our* trespasses. (my italics. PB.)

76.  *And Love said:* Judge not yet you be judged.

77.  *And Love said:* Peace, you say. I am the *totality*
     of it.

78.  *And Love said:* In seeing you now in this time
     and place, I have glimpsed Eternity. For you will
     never wither and fade; never die.

79.  *And Love said:* You make me sound so
     complicated when I am really so simple.
     The further you stray from me the more
     complicated I get.

80.  *And Love said:* When I am here every day seems
     like a new beginning. It *is* a new beginning
     because I've never moved.

81.  *And Love said:* Let no man tell you what love is,
     it is too vast a subject, or maybe it is too
     simple.

82. **And Love said:** Oh, do not ask, 'What is it?'
                         Let us go and make our visit.

83. **And Love said:**
    Do I dare
    Disturb the universe?
    In a minute there is time
    For decisions and revisions
    Which a minute will reverse.

84. **And Love said:**
    There is shadow under this red rock
    (Come in under the shadow of this red rock),
    And I will show you something different from
                                          either
    Your shadow at morning striding behind you
    Or your shadow at evening rising to meet you
    I will show you *love* in a handful of dust.

85. **And Love said:** Your behaviour around children
    and your teaching of children is a reflection of
    who *you* are. But the character is already *with*
    the child from long ago. No matter how you
    behave and how you teach, try and bring out
    that that is good and tolerating that that is bad
    and all else will fall into balance.

86. **And Love said:** The *love* of God is the
    beginning of knowledge: but the foolish despise
    wisdom and instruction. But in the end come
    to Love because Love is all there is.

87. **And Love said:** Justice is conformity to truth.
    Truth is balance. Balance is Love.

88.  *And Love said:* It is not a matter of what you
     love and who you love but the manner in *which*
     you love.

89.  *And Love said:* You can love an adoring audience
     but can you love the individuals that constitute
     an audience?

90.  *And Love said:* If an individual smells, or is ugly
     to behold, or behaves in a manner that disturbs
     you, or is *all* of these things. Try to love what
     they are not. On the other hand they might
     find *you* offensive.

91.  *And Love said:* By my very nature you will see
     *all* things reflected in me and *all* things reflected
     in yourself. They are the same.

92.  *And Love said:* You will see later on that all
     creatures and all that is, is you.

93.  *And Love said:* Even if you are the worst sinner
     amongst all sinners, you will cross all sin by the
     boat of knowledge (Love) alone.

94.  *And Love said:* Verily, there exists no purifier
     on earth equal to knowledge (Love). A person
     who becomes perfect in yoga (spiritual practice)
     finds it within themselves in the fullness of time.

95.  *And Love said:* Though they may not believe in
     a God, or *any* God. Just through the acts of
     kindness, forgiveness and Love they *are* God.
     They live the very nature of God. They just
     don't put labels on it, that's all.

96.  *And Love said:* To realise the suffering, poverty and misery of human kind; to realise the cruelty perpetrated against animal kind. To share in compassion and tearfulness *is not enough!* DO something about it, no matter how little.

97.  *And Love said:* Unswerving devotion to Love through all the spiritual practises of non-separation , resorting to solitude and aversion for company, always being devoted to spiritual knowledge, perception of the aim of the knowledge of Love - all this is declared to be knowledge and all that that is contrary to this is ignorance.

98.  *And Love said:* For pity's sake, have fun along the way, enjoy what you achieve whether you achieve a little or a lot. Slow down! It's not a race to the end. There is no end!

99.  *And Love said:* If all you have to offer is your strength, then that is enough. If all you have to offer is your will, then that is enough. If all you have to offer is Me, then that is enough. For all things are then added to you.

100. *And Love said:* I am the Grail (Truth) that all seek, the vessel that overflows and keeps on overflowing. But you will *never* contain me.

101. *And Love said:* I remain an abstraction until you can understand me, and in understanding me suddenly I am an abstraction once again. Do you see?

102. **And Love said:** Neither be cynical about *Me;* for in the face of all aridity and disenchantment, *I am* as perennial as the grass.

103. **And Love said:** You are a child of the universe no less than the trees and the stars; you have a right to be here.

104. **And Love said:** Love is a shower of leaves raining from an autumn sky.

105. **And Love said:** I am the friendship that survives all pain.

106. **And Love said:** I am the acceptance and the surrender of the force within. I *am* the force!

107. **And Love said:** I am the contentment that comes from doing what you believe is right; and having the courage to admit that perhaps you were wrong.

108. **And Love said:** When a soul relinquishing all work surrenders themselves to me, it is then that I like to magnify them most. Attaining immortality they are then fit for oneness with me.

109. **And Love said:** Even if a very wicked person worships me with devotion to none else, they should be regarded as good, for they have rightly resolved.

110. **And Love said:** The excitement and joy of going home with you with all the rules and regulations

in balence, knowing that I/we won't need them anymore. What more can I ask?

111.   *And Love said:* Time is your friend not your enemy. Why do you spend *your* time chasing it when everything is as it should be?

112.   Time? Pahh! When God made Time he made an awful lot of it!

113.   *And Love said:* Do not, in your angry and depressive moods, forget who I am. It is so easy to forget me when stark emotion takes you out of my reach.

114.   *And Love said:* Are you so proud that you use me as a weapon? That is not the real me but an imposter!

115.   *And Love said:* I have many faces but only *you* know who I am.

116.   *And Love said:* I allow you to be who you truly are. Whether you choose a negative or positive stance. In the positive mirror I am reflected as all that is joyful, whilst in the negative mirror I seem to disappear. I am *always* there but *you* choose not to see me.

117.   *And Love said:* And when you say:"It brings out the old spark in you." Don't you mean to say: "It brings out the spark that was covered, temporarily, beyond time and space?" There was never an *old* spark or a *new* spark.

*I* will not pretend that the path to me is an easy
one. I will not pretend that it is paved with
gold. When you realize that what happens to
you is a result of *your* making; and when
you also realise that *I* do not *judge* you as
a result of this, then you will be a person of
*self-realisation.* But not yet!

118. **And Love said:** Love some one! In God's name
*love* some one. For this is the bread of the
inner life, without which a part of you will
starve and die. Part of you will cease to exist.

119. **And Love Said:** Tell me truly, have you been *so*
hurt by another human being that you hide
yourself away? So embittered that you do not
allow yourself to love? A sign of strength is to
admit to your weaknesses. Is *this* your
strength, not allowing love to come near?

120. **And Love Said:** A balance between black and
white gives you grey: it is the balance between
the *variations* of grey that gives you the
photograph, variations of love that gives you
the true picture.

121. **And Love Said:** The camera also tells lies.
Love is the sum-total of it, **all** of it. A
negative balanced by a positive. Together
they make a whole. You do not believe me?
Try it for yourself. Let love take the reigns
and ride roughshod over you. Give it a try.
You have nothing to lose, except face. Even
that compared with your **true** hurt is a little
price to pay.

122. *And Love Said:* Don't hide behind your pain,
don't use pain as a shield.

123. *And Love Said:* Never expect something in
return for good deeds done. Forget them.
They'll return to you when you least expect.

124. *And Love Said:* I remove the candles from the
Altar. Instead, I light one in every heart so
that it will shine and burn and search for life in
all the dead places.

125. *And Love Said:* In that day there shall be
forgotten things, things that never have been
because they are forgotten, and will never be
remembered again.

126. *And Love Said:* I am the revelation that *all seek.*
I am there for the asking. Demand what is
rightfully yours!

127. *And Love Said:* Love is harmony, love is
unselfish. A person will do things for love which
he/she would not do for any money.

128. *And Love Said:* You rise and stretch your wings.
Not for a single day, but forever.

129. *And Love Said:* Greed is a kind of laziness.

130. *And Love Said:* Don't concern your new self
with that that is past.

And do not grieve it. They will catch
up *transformed..*

131.   *And Love said:* Search, search, my darling, lest
I be standing unaware, looking for you the
other way.

132.   *And Love said:* You are forever, and so am I.

133.   *And Love said:* No kiss is wasted, Johnnie
Blunt, to see embodied in you only the need to
love and the ability to love, puts us all to
shame. *(a child with Downs Syndrome)*

134.   *And Love said:* Death is just a blip in the
continuation of consciousness. The difference is
that you leave those who mourn to those who
welcome.

135 .*And Love said:* If you try hard but still don't
succeed. Your power lies not in your failure but
in your *intent* to succeed.

136.   *And Love said:* And however you are
afflicted, whether it be mentally, emotionally, or
physically, remember this: you are the sum-total
of all that went before, in *this* life and in
others; and I still love you.

137.   *And Love said:* There is no separation. No line
can be drawn between one thing and another,
either in time or in space.

# SECTION THREE

———

138. *And Love said:* Balance is what is required here,
Balance and Harmony, or you will become Earth-
addicts. Addiction is a terrible thing and if you
want to leave this beautiful earth at some time
addiction to it is what will bind you.

139. *And Love said:* Pride is linked to loss-of-face,
stubbornness and ego. Yes, it all comes down to
ego. When Balance is applied then 'letting-go'
takes care of itself. Who said that some bruising
will not occur along the way? I didn't.

140. *And Love said:* Everything 'new' upon the earth
is taken up by Karma and applied accordingly.
The law of Karma (cause and effect) is perfect.
Just as my love for you is perfect. Besides which
there *is* nothing new.

141. *And Love said:* Work together for the benefit of
all peoples.

142. *And Love said:* Give assistance and kindness
wherever needed.

143. *And Love said:* Dedicate a share of your efforts,
no matter how small, to the greater good.

144. *And Love said:* Take full responsibility for your
actions.

145. *And Love said:* Karma is the great leveler and
the bringer of Self-Justice.

146. *And Love said:* All that you do is witnessed by
Self.

147. *And Love said:* Whatever you can do, or dream you can, begin it: boldness has genius, power and magic in it; begin it now!

148. *And Love said:* Justice is a two edged sword: be careful where you stick it.

149. *And Love said:* Time is an illusion, a yard-stick for measuring out your life. Use it sensibly whilst you are here, but never let it run away with you for it will trap you and become a reality.

150. *And Love said:* Hate brings into play all that I am not. Hate binds you in bonds of agony. Only I can set you free.

151. *And Love said:* Hate blinds you to what is truly real. Generation after generation are *taught* to hate each other. Have the courage to break the cycle and others will surely follow.

152. *And Love said:* The very act of patience will attract attention. Be prepared to wait, for it is highly contagious.

153. *And Love said:* Patience is the master of time.

154. *And Love said:* Laughter and good humour speaks all languages. Try it.

155. *And Love said:* If you draw attention to yourself, be prepared to back it up with justification and truth. If you do not then be prepared for trouble of your own making.

156. *And Love said:* Anger is Truth out of control.

157. *And Love said:* Nothing is lost unless you want it so.

158. *And Love said:* From your heart centre radiates all the love you will ever know. To access it, either in thought or in deed, open wide and say: Ommmm...

159. *And Love said:* Laughter is the panacea of all suffering. If you can just break a smile through all your agony then you are half-way there.

160. *And Love said:* The label of hero or heroine is false if what you do is a reflex. If what you do is genuinely heroic and you suffer, either mentally or physically, as a consequence knowing full-well the consequences, *that* is being brave *that* is true heroism. But show humility on *both* counts and I(Love)will hand out the medals in person.

161. *And Love said:* I exist elsewhere too: the many regions of the heart, the mountainous heights of your soul, the lower slopes of your spirit. I am everywhere. But where do *you* search for me? A lover's kiss and embrace? The addict's needle? A gourmet's meal? I am neither of these. Elusive I may be but then that's part of the game, isn't it?

162. *And Love said:* Guilt is an act of programming. To kill is not good, to save a life is good. Where do you function between the two? On the one

hand you *know* it is wrong to kill, even though
that person killed your brother. On the other
hand to save a life is *good,* even though it is the
person who killed your brother. Were you to
take the life of this person would you feel guilt
or revenge? Revenge, you see, is part of
programming and thus the sense of guilt is out
of control. To feel guilty is an emotional *safety
valve.* The lesson here is always keep a sense of
*balance* where guilt is concerned. Your goal
should be a detached unconditional-love for *all*
your emotions. When you have achieved that
then you will have come *home to me!*

163. *And Love said:* A psychopath is one who has no
sense of guilt. None. They are detached from it
and therefore do vile things with impunity. Guilt
is a necessary evil but a *balanced* guilt is what is
required. A sensible guilt.

164. *And Love said:* There is *hope* for the
psychopath, if they realise that life is
eternal, that in reality they cannot destroy
*anything.*

165. *And Love said:* Go beyond the concept of 'New'
and you will come to me.

166. *And Love said:* If you approach pain with fear it
intensifies. If you approach pain *without* fear
then it only hurts.

167. *And Love said:* Poems found locked in a drawer
reveal the inner *you.* Poems for publication reveal
the inner *you* but, by their nature, are
disguised in poetry.

168. *And Love said:* The poet enters worlds that we
can read and follow. Love enters worlds that
even poetry cannot follow. Yet all are welcome.

169. *And Love said:* Greed is a thing of *this* world:
either a hoarder or a power-monger. Both are
essentially the same. They are addicted to what
they hoard just as they become addicted with the
power they hold over others. The lesson is the
same: let them be mindful of the Truth of
eternity. *Everyone* is a potentional creator.

170. *And Love said:* Give me a break. Give me a
chance. See what I can do.

171. *And Love said:* You searched for me, and you
found me; and so you did cross the threshold.
The *intent of infinity* told me to look for
someone like you. I found you, thus crossing the
threshold myself.

172. *And Love said:* I understood with unequalled
clarity what he (Love) was explaining. I didn't
have to ask him for clarifications. My keenness
of thought should have surprised me, but it
didn't at all. I knew at that moment that I had
always been crystal clear, merely playing dumb
for someone else's benefit.

173. *And Love said:* I did that to you at the bus
depot because I wanted to stop your barrage of
*me, me, me, me.* I wanted you to find me
and cut the crap.

174. *And Love said:* Don Juan went on explaining that
the moment one crosses a peculiar threshold in
*infinity,* or, as in my case, unwittingly,
everything that happens to one from then on is
no longer exclusively in one's own domain, but
enters into the realm of *infinity.* (divine love)

175. *And Love said:* There's no pondering,
wondering, or speculation. They *know* that all
they have is the possibility of merging with the
*intent of infinity,* and they just do it.

176. *And Love said:* You have to, finally, kill the
monster that your senses (ego) have created. You
can do this, for instance, when you feel that
your world is collapsing about you. And indeed it
is!  But collapsing in-as-much as the 'old'
welcoming the 'new'. You will find that you no
longer have the urge to prove this-or-that,
either physically, emotionally or spiritually. But
this is not without much pain. But at the end of
it you will be free! I will be with you every step
of the way. You may feel that I have deserted
you. Nothing is further from the truth.

177. *And Love said:* Conquer Love and you have
everything, there is no more. There is only
Love. Learn to Love unconditionally.

178. *And Love said:* Do you remember me? Do you
remember the way it was? Do you remember the
days when we lived in harmony? It can be that
way again.

179. *And Love said:* But you know of Love and you know how to Love. What else is there to know? It is this that will sustain and guide you in the days to come.

180. *And Love said:* People will take one glance and be transformed; others will need to be hit over the head with a concrete mallet because they are so asleep in themselves! Their spiritual amnesia is many, many metres thick!

181. *And Love said:* To love without desiring. To want without wanting. To remember without remembering. This is *all* of it.

182. *And Love said:* Infinity has no name yet it pulls you to itself relentlessly.

183. *And Love said:* Balance is wisdom, wisdom is justice, justice is balance. The heart contains all three.

184. *And Love said:* Leave not a trace of you behind, not a thing but the bones of which the earth designed you. Settle your debts, either spiritually, morally or monetary, say your goodbyes and quietly but with dignity leave.

185. *And Love said:* You have left many a signpost to Freedom (love). Now let other's carry Truth's flag and leave you to explore that Freedom.

186. *And Love said:* There will come a time when you leave; out of the earth's karmic lure towards infinity. Toward me.

187. *And Love said:* There has to come a time when Freedom (love) swallows you up.

188. *And Love said:* Love is the glue that hold's together every universe, of which there is no end.

189. *And Love said:* Life on other planets? Of course there is! Do you think that you are so grand? Do you think that you are the centre of creation? Nothing *was* created, just brought together.

190. *And Love said:* You have to open your minds to God (Love) to expand consciousness, to you. Every grain of sand, every hair on your head, is God. All is awareness. Everything. There is no separation, there is no time and space; there is only NOW.

191. *And Love said:* It is a responsibility to spread truth and light, it is the greatest joy; but sometimes it is very painful, and of course, you will all get rebuked occasionally – maybe even laughed at sometimes. But we simply carry on quietly in our own way, doing our job, just as I do mine.

192. *And Love said:* Please hold on to love, please! Practice love and the transition is so easy. Love is not easy. If you have love in your hearts, you could almost say anything and people would respond to you because love is truth. The language between lovers is crazy, but it is wonderful. So it is with the love of God.

193. *And Love said:* Please hold the concept of love
alway in your minds. It is such a vast, yet such
a simple subject. You know very well that it is
the ego and the intellect that makes love so
complicated but in essence it is so simple. The
Universe is simple. The whole idea of the
Godhead is simple. Because that's all it is: an
*idea.* And one day, when you have attained a
degree of enlightment, you will look back and
you will laugh. And your voice will ring out
through the Universe, joined by others who have
also felt this realzitation of the Divine. And you
will say "How could I have been so stupid, that I
did not see the simplicity of this Universe?"

194. *And Love said:* Cherish *all* creation, all of it.
There is nothing that you cannot leave out!

195. *And Love said:* Mistreat an animal and you will
mistreat yourself.

196. *And Love said:* Do animals have an after-life?
You can bet on it. Why should you have all the
luck. You're not *that* special.

197. *And Love said:* You may have been made in
God's image, but do you really *know* the image
of God? The Infinite? What arrogance is this that
you can display so blatantly that you *know?* You
may as well describe a pile of sand.

198. *And Love said:* Everything that creeps and
crawls has its place. Let no man tell you
otherwise as you spread your poison on the
ground.

# SECTION FOUR

———

199. *And Love said:* Children are our future,
they always were. Firstly, teach them about
me. If you can't conceive of that then teach
them to be kind. Kindness is a requisite.

200. *And Love said:* Animals are only demanding of
our affection, understanding and patience. They
are what they are: sentient beings, just like you.
No more, no less.

201. *And Love said:* Don't you think it strange that
human life demands beginnings and endings.
Energy, in the form of love, finds it equally
strange.

202. *And Love said:* I am waiting for that beauty
whereby all that is now regarded as beautiful will
seem tawdry and vulgar. And men will discard
their shabby ideals in shame, as they will throw
away their outwarn ways of thought and feeling,
emerging from their prisons and tombs into the
light of day.

203. *And Love said:* I am warm to welcome all those
who, dissatisfied with what passes for truth and
beauty and who have been given stones instead of
bread, in their restlessness and emptiness, are
also looking, listening and waiting.

204. *And Love said:* Yet what is it but the Dawn that
in its purity and power, sensed but not yet seen,
already breathes of the books to be written, the
songs to be sung, the truths to be given,

the beauty to be unveiled for the awakening of mankind and the healing of nations.

205. *And Love said:* Remember that you carry this treasure within you that was yours even before you were born. It was there as you grew within the womb. It will be with you until you depart from this world and after.

206. *And Love said:* In fact as your need grows, it will become more valuable.

207. *And Love said:* When all the familier lines of your life have been erased. And new challenges make  you vulnerable and afraid. Trust that the gift of the Unknown is courage and love.

208. *And Love said:* But what I have to give you is intangible as it is invisible.

209. *And Love said:* In the worlds eyes I am old. But I tell you my heart is young, for it holds the soul of a child whose cradle rocks gently to the tides of heaven.

210. *And Love said:* Death is the homing motion of the soul.

211. *And Love said: Nothing* is lost. All is given and taken back and given again.

212. *And Love said:* Honesty is truly the best policy. Even a white lie told in the best interests of the recipient must, at some stage, be rectified, when the recipient is strong enough to take it.

213. *And Love said:* The Truth (Love) is what you
deem it to be in the moment of your Truth.
Then it broadens out and becomes something that
is a mere aspect, a shadow, of your former
Truth. That is if you are a *true* follower of
Truth.

214. *And Love said:* Children dream in their innocence
and *naturally* live in the moment. Woe betide
*anyone* that destroys that innocence and forces
that child to live, prematurely, for tomorrow.

215. *And Love said:* Teach your children kindness if
nothing else, kindness for *all* creatures. For
kindness contains all that is necessary for a
happy life. It does not matter that they don't
believe in a God or Gods or, for that matter,
eternity. For when it comes for them to die and
they are afraid, then *I* step in. For I *am*
kindness.

216. *And Love said:* Bend a little, like a tree in the
wind. You do not have to change your character
anymore than a tree changes *its* character. But
for pity's sake *BEND!*

217. *And Love said:* You *have* to forgive in the light
of eternity or you go on hating for eternity.

218. *And Love said:* Trust me, I am Doctor Love.

219. *And Love said:* Each little deed or thought or
word of love is stored away for eternity.

220. **_And Love said:_** We are able to be free of time and free of space, free of the world that hangs on space and time.

221. **_And Love said:_** It is the inner light of all that makes the world beautiful: like a flame shining through coloured glass, which otherwise would be dead and lifeless, but which now gleams and sparkles in every form of loveliness.

222. **_And Love said:_** We come here in order to re-learn it, (love) but essentially to love _ourselves._ How else can we radiate love?

223. **_And Love said:_** Material things/objects, no matter how beautiful and desirable must not gain power over you. For in the end you have to leave this planet, and them. Think of them as energies, frequencies, memories, and then let them go.

224. **_And Love said:_** Where you go I will go. What you do I will do. What you think I will think. And if after all the journeying; if after all the doing; if after all the thinking you still cannot recognize Me. Then we have it all to go, do and think again. Because I will **never** leave you, nor forsake you. You cannot shake me off just like that.

225. **_And Love said:_** In the autumn of my years when things begin to stiffen and stifle, when I can only eat fruit trifle and rifle through what might have been. The scene is not to look back and lack the means to make it right. For lovc is forever

youthful and truthful, never trite. For as the
shadows grow long and you sing love's song,
though silent on your lips, and mouth the words:
*LOVE*. And it roars and it roars and it roars
down the years until you cry for joy and say:
*this* is what it is! *this* is what it is!

226.  *And Love said:* The solution to retribution is
resolution...and you go on from there!

227.  *And Love said:* Instant karma? The more you
leave karma alone the more it leaves *you* alone.
In other words: if you are kind to *all* creation
this produces instant karma. Give it a while to
kick-in though; others may have different ideas.
Be consistent in your kindness.

228.  *And Love said:* Karma goes round and round
and round and round and round and round and
round and (boring isn't it) round and...Had
enough pain yet? Then *change*. *Get off the
roundabout!* To be dizzy is to be confused. You
*can* do it. What was it? In that film? You know
the one, where the central character cries out:
FREEDOM! FREEDOM! FREEDOM! FREEDOM!

229.  *And Love said:* To abstain from killing.

300.  *And Love said:* To abstain from stealing.

301.  *And Love said:* To abstain from cheating.

302.  *And Love said:* To abstain from lying.

303.  *And Love said:* To abstain from liquor.

304. *And Love said:* Right understanding, free from superstition and delusion.

305. *And Love said:* Right thought; high and worthy of the intelligent.

306. *And Love said:* Right Speech; kindly; open, truthful.

307. *And Love said:* Right Actions; peaceful, honest, pure.

308. *And Love said:* Right Livelihood: not bringing hurt or danger to a living being.

309. *And Love said:* Right Effort; in self-training and in self-control.

310. *And Love said:* Right Mindfulness; the active, watchful mind.

311. *And Love said:* Right Concentration; in deep meditation on the realities of life.

312. *And Love said:* Give charity to the deserving.

313. *And Love said:* Observe the precepts of morality.

314. *And Love said:* Cultivate and develop good thoughts.

315. *And Love said:* Render service and attend on others.

316. *And Love said:* Honour and nurse parents and
elders.

317. *And Love said:* Give a share of your merits to
others.

318. *And Love said:* Hear the doctrine of the divine.

319. *And Love said:* Preach the doctrine of the divine.

320. *And Love said:* Rectify your faults.

321. *And Love said:* Do not seek revenge though
every nerve and sinew cries out for it. Let
the natural law of cause and effect take care of
it, allow karma to do its work. Do you want to
step off life's merry-go-round of pain or don't
you? Make up your mind. Still, you have eternity
to do that.

323. *And Love said:* It is thought better when
families: brother against brother, brother against
sister, husband against wife and quarrels of that
nature, that a mediator be employed. A healer, a
wiseman or woman, a person of balence.
    There should be no shame in this. That is
what people of wisdom, love and balance do. If
they do not then you have chosen badly. If you
have chosen wisely then the mediator will restore
peace to the situation, heal the wounds of your
discomfort; though he or she may have to spend
much time with you. Be prepared for that.

324. *And Love said:* They who recognize the existence of suffering, its cause, its remedy, and its cessation, has fathomed the Four Noble Truths. Then they will walk in the right path.

325. *And Love said:* You shall love your neighbour as yourself. There is no other commandment greater than this.

326. *And Love said:* It is easier for a camel to go through the eye of a needle than for a rich man to enter the kingdom of God.

327. *And Love said:* But many that are first shall be last; and the last shall be first. for many are called, but few are chosen.

328. *And Love said:* Heaven and earth will pass away: but my words will not pass away.

329. *And Love said:* A new commandment I give you, that you love one another as I have loved you.

330. *And Love said:* They who keep my commandments love me: and they who love me shall be loved by my Father and I will love them, and I will manifest myself to them.

331. *And Love said:* When you give alms, let your left hand know what your right hand does. Your alms be in secret and your Father who sees it in secret shall reward you openly.

332. *And Love said:* Whosoever saves his life shall lose it: and whosoever loses his life for my sake

will find it. For what does a man profit if he gains the whole world, and loses his own soul.

333. *And Love said:* It has been said: an eye for an eye and a tooth for a tooth. But I say, do not resist evil. Whoever smites you on your right cheek, turn to him the other also.

334. *And Love said:* Take heed how you hear; for whosoever has, to him shall be given; and whosoever has not, from him shall be taken even that which he seems to have.

335. *And Love said:* Spontaneous and random acts of kindness, no matter how small. Or large, come to that.

336. *And Love said:* Friendship *is* those little acts of kindness. Plus confidential intimacy. Shared silence.  Friendship you can rage against because there is no one else around on which you can vent your wrath, and *still* they are there for you no matter how out-of-line you may be.

337. *And Love said:* You, whose nature is mercy and compassion, whose Being is all peace, Father, Creator and sustainer of our lives, pour on the whole on humanity your healing, your comfort, your peace and  your love, and unite us all in your perfect Being.

338. *And Love said:* Everything comes to they who wait, but a little nudge now and again cannot go amiss.

# SECTION FIVE

———

339. *And Love said:* Break the silence between you with laughter. If you can't tell a joke then laugh anyway. Laughter is infectious but not a serious infection.

340. *And Love said:* You do not understand our Prayers when we address the Sun, Moon and Winds, you have judged us without understanding only because our Prayers are different. We are able to live in harmony with *all* of Nature. All of Nature is within us and we are part of *all* Nature. (my italics. PB)

341. *And Love said:* God sleeps in the minerals; dreams in the flowers; but in man he *knows*, He is awake. (my italics. PB)

342. *And Love said:* There is nothing covered that shall not be uncovered, neither known that is not known. Whatever you speak in darkness will be heard in the light. And that that you speak behind closed doors will be proclaimed from the roof-tops.

343. *And Love said:* Kindness has its own reward, so does badness.

344. *And Love said:* Always remember you're unique, just like everyone else.

345. *And Love said:* If ignorance is bliss, where are all the happy people?

346. *And Love said:* Puritanism is the fear that someone, somewhere may be happy.

347. **And Love said:** The best way to predict the future is to be kind to one another.

348. **And Love said:** We are not conscious of our own unconsciousness.

349. **And Love said:** Those who are patient in adversity and forgive wrongs are the doers of excellence.

350. **And Love said:** Speak to men according to their mental capacities, for if you speak all things to all men, some cannot understand you and so fall into errors.

351. **And Love said:** It is your own conduct which will lead you to reward or punishment, as if you had been destined for it.

352. **And Love said:** When you go and visit the sick, comfort their grief and say: "You will get better and live long." This saying will not prevent what is predestined, but it will bring peace to their soul.

353. **And Love said:** To be alone is better than to have a bad companion; and a good companion is better than being alone; and dictating the good is better than keeping silence; and silence is better than dictating evil.

354. **And Love said:** God enjoins you to treat women well, for they are your mothers, daughters and aunts.

355. ***And Love said:*** Forgive them who wrong you: join them who cut you off; do good to those who do evil to you, and speak the truth although it be against oneself.

356. ***And Love said:*** Let no one judge between two parties in a suit when they are in a rage.

357. ***And Love said:*** Resistance is pain.

358. ***And Love said:*** Believe in your self but keep it to your self.

359. ***And Love said:*** Trouble is a tunnel through which we must pass, not a brick wall against which we must break out heads.

360. ***And Love said:*** Each player must accept the cards life deals him or her. But once they are in hand, he or she alone must decide how to play the cards in order to win the game.

361. ***And Love said:*** Courage is the art of being the only one who knows you're scared to death.

362. ***And Love said:*** Sometimes the worst thing God can do for you is to grant you your wishes.

363. ***And Love said:*** Flattery rarely hurts unless you inhale.

364. ***And Love said:*** Prayer was not invented. It was born in the first sigh, the first joy, the first sorrow of the human heart.

365.  *And Love said:* Days are not days, you know,
but eternal steps toward me.

366.  *And Love said:* The value lies not in the length
of days but in the use of them.

367.  *And Love said:* You cannot travel on the path
before you have become the path itself.

368.  *And Love said:* A spirit filled with truth must
needs direct its actions to the final goal.

369.  *And Love said:* Only the ignorant person
becomes angry. The wise person understands.

370.  *And Love said:* Learn true joy and you will
embrace the Infinite.

371.  *And Love said:* Luck may sometimes help; work
always helps. If you do not worry about a
misfortune for three years, it will become a
blessing.

372.  *And Love said:* For life, with all it yields of joy
And woe, and hope and fear,
Is just one chance of the prize
Of learning love.

373.  *And Love said:* A person can only do what they
can do. But if they do that each day they can
sleep at night and do it again the next day.

374.  *And Love said:* Life is eternal and love immortal,
and death is only a horizon, and a horizon is
nothing save the limit of our sight.

375. *And Love said:* You can't live on hope, but it should be on the menu.

376. *And Love said:* When you least expect it happiness comes tugging on your line, and you know nothing about fishing.

377. *And Love said:* Eternity cannot live on a diet of yesterdays and tomorrows. That's why it created men and women: so that it can understand what indigestion is.

378. *And Love said:* Perhaps, just perhaps. No, no. Maybe, just maybe.... Ah, to hell with it: you *were* right and I was wrong. There, I've said it, and I didn't feel a thing!

379. *And Love said:* Love is a doing thing!

380. *And Love said:* What is it about a fire that draws us to hearth and home? What lies buried deep? Even the most unsavoury of us need that comfort. But it lies even deeper than that, beyond comfort, warmth, and food. It is a sense of wanting to *belong* to something. A flickering in the flame itself, wanting to *become* the fire, wanting to welcome those who come for its warmth, who, up until that moment, are lost.

381. *And Love said:* Unless you dance you know not what cometh to pass.

382. *And Love said:* And when love speaks the voice of all the gods makes heaven drowsy with the harmony.

383. *And Love said:* Lord, help me to keep my big
     mouth shut until I know what I am talking about.

384. *And Love said:* Questions followed by an answer
     until there are *no* questions: the question
     becomes the answer, the answer becomes the
     question.

385. *And Love said:* The atheist will say they don't
     believe in a god. Surely they have to believe in
     something. That's it, they believe in something!
     Well, it's a start, for goodness sake! '

386. *And Love said:* Cast your bread upon the waters
     and it will come back buttered!

387. *And Love said:* Instead of seeing the rug pulled
     from under us, we can learn to dance on a
     shifting carpet.

388. *And Love said:* Walk with me, even if it's only
     the length of the room and I'll show you the hole
     in the carpet and much, much more!

389. *And Love said:* However you are affected during
     the course of this life, remember this: you are
     the sum total of all that went before. And I still
     love you.

390. *And Love said:* Every blade of grass has its
     angel that bends over it and whispers, "Grow
     grow."

391. *And Love said:* Every tree crawls with life,
     that's not counting the tree itself which is well

aware of the things that crawl.

392. *And Love said:* Don't try and push time. Time is your friend not your enemy and tends to push back!

393. *And Love said:* Whatever is left out in your knowledge of self will keep growing until you can clutch the stars...and then some.

394. *And Love said:* And of course you except that every snow flake is individually crafted, has its own unique idiosyncrasy, babbling to one another about this and that, raging, one to the other, about the art of being different....until the thaw sets in.

395. *And Love said:* Love has no direction but toward itself. And where does it go from there? The answer is up to you, surely.

396. *And Love said:* And so the journey of love comes to an end, or is it a new beginning? No matter, because if you argue the point then you've failed to see the point.

397. *And Love Said:* The anguish that desire brings, the separation (yet there *is* no seperation) that the lessons of the soul bring. Ah, but the adventure is worth all the pain, isn't it?

398. *And Love Said:* Until you separate out and start the journey on your own you will not know what it is like. That separation, that segment IS YOU!

399. ***And Love Said:*** In the tiniest corner of the human mind there dwells curiosity...for Me.

400. ***And Love said:*** Remember not only the men of good will, but also those of ill will. But do not only remember all the suffering they have inflicted on us, remember the fruits we brought, thanks to the suffering, our comradeship, our loyalty, out humility, the courage, the generosity, the greatness of heart which has grown out of all this. And when they come to judgement, let all the fruits that we have borne be their forgiveness.

401. ***And Love said****:* It is *forgiveness* that lays the dust of pain, forgiveness and love. And when you lay awake at night opening all the old wounds, settling all the old scores, it is these two things and only these two things that make it right and just. They are, after all, the same thing. Who said that it was easy to forgive. But you *must*. It is the only way forward.

402. ***And Love said:*** A stray dog was to bring comfort to a war-field *medical team*. He became particully close to a young surgeon who used to give him tit-bits. You could say that they adored each other. The dog's tail would go into spasm every time they saw each other. One day the dog went missing. The young surgeon hunted and hunted for him but reasoned that he had found his true owner at last. The surgeon put it to the back of his mind.

　　When called to a medical tent one day there stretched out, his stomach open and pinned, was the dog. He whimpered his recognition

and attempted to wag his tail. The surgeon
was shocked beyond belief at what he saw.
The dog looked up at him and licked his
hand.

403. ***And Love said:*** You can never come to the end
of love, it just goes on and on and on
and...Boring? I never said love was boring! I just
said that it goes on and on and on and on and....

404. ***And Love said:*** There is no more other than the
more you make and the more you make is
endless!

405. ***And Love (finally) said:*** There *is* no finality.

# INDEX

# INDEX CONTINUED.

# APPENDIX.

31. Quote taken from the book *THE ART OF DREAMING by Carlus Castaneda*. Published by *Aquarian*. An imprint of Harper/Collins.

61. Taken from the poem *The Invitation*. Published by *MOUNTAIN DREAMING* from the book: *Dreams of Desire*.

63. Taken from the poem *The Invitation.*

82. (extract) T.S. Eliot:
83. (extract) T.S. Eliot:
84. Taken from *THE WASTE LAND & FOUR QUARTETS by T.S. Eliot*. Published by Faber and Faber.

102. Extract taken from *THE DESIDERATA OF HAPPINESS by Max Ehrmann*. Published by Blue Mountain Arts. Boulder, Colorado, USA.
103. Extract from *THE DESIDERATA OF HAPPINESS.*
119. Extract from *THE DESIDERATA OF HAPPINESS.*

124. Part of *BREAKING THROUGH by Derek Neville*. Published by The Mitre Press, London.
125. Extract from.....
128. Extract from....
131. Extract from....
137. Extract from....

171. Extracts from *THE ACTIVE SIDE OF INFINITY by Carlos Castaneda*. Published by Thorsons. An Imprint of HarperCollins *Publishers.*
172. Don Juan Matus (extract)
173. Don Juan Matus (extract)

## APPENDIX CONTINUED

174. Don Juan Matus.(extract)
175. Don Juan Matus.(extract)

176. Extract from *JOEB-SERVANT OF GAIA*
     Published by Symbol Creations.
177. Extract from.....
178. Extract from.....
179. Extract from.....
180. Extract from.....
188. Extract from....
189. Extract from....
190. Extract from....
191. Extract from....
192. Extract from....
193. Extract from....

202. Extract from *THE RIVER THAT KNOWS THE
     WAY.* Edited by *Stephanie Sorrell and Illustrated
     by Hanne Jahr.* Published by The Science of
     Thought Review.
203. Extract from....
204. Extract from....
205. Extract from:
206. Extract from....
207. Extract from....
208. Extract from....
209. Extract from....

219. Extract from *THE GARDEN OF SILENCE and
     PUT OFF THY SHOES by Derek Neville.*
     Published by Arthur James Ltd.
220. Extract from....
221. Extract from....

400. This prayer was found on a piece of Wrapping
     Paper near the body of a dead child in

## *APPENDIX CONTINUED*

Ravensbruck Nazi Concentration Camp, where 92, 000 women and children died.